BUILDING LANDMARKS

BRIDGES, TUNNELS AND BUILDINGS

Architecture and Design
Children's Engineering Books

BABY PROFESSOR

EDUCATION KIDS

Speedy Publishing LLC

40 E. Main St. #1156

Newark, DE 19711

www.speedypublishing.com

Copyright 2017

In this book, we're going to talk about how bridges, tunnels, and buildings are designed and built. So, let's get right to it!

Architects and construction teams face unique challenges depending on whether they are designing and building bridges, tunnels, or buildings.

PULTENEY BRIDGE

BRIDGES

Historians think that ancient peoples may have gotten the idea for building bridges from fallen trees. They noticed how the trees made it possible for them to cross shallow waterways. Since the first primitive wooden bridges, the design of bridges has gone from stone arches to huge suspension structures. They are pounded by wind, water, and traffic all day, every day, so they have to be built very well to be safe.

HOW BRIDGES BALANCE FORCES

Gravity on Earth is always pulling things down. A skyscraper has a foundation as well as ground underneath it to support its structure, but a bridge that spans a waterway is very different. The large horizontal structure of a bridge, called its deck, doesn't have any support directly under it.

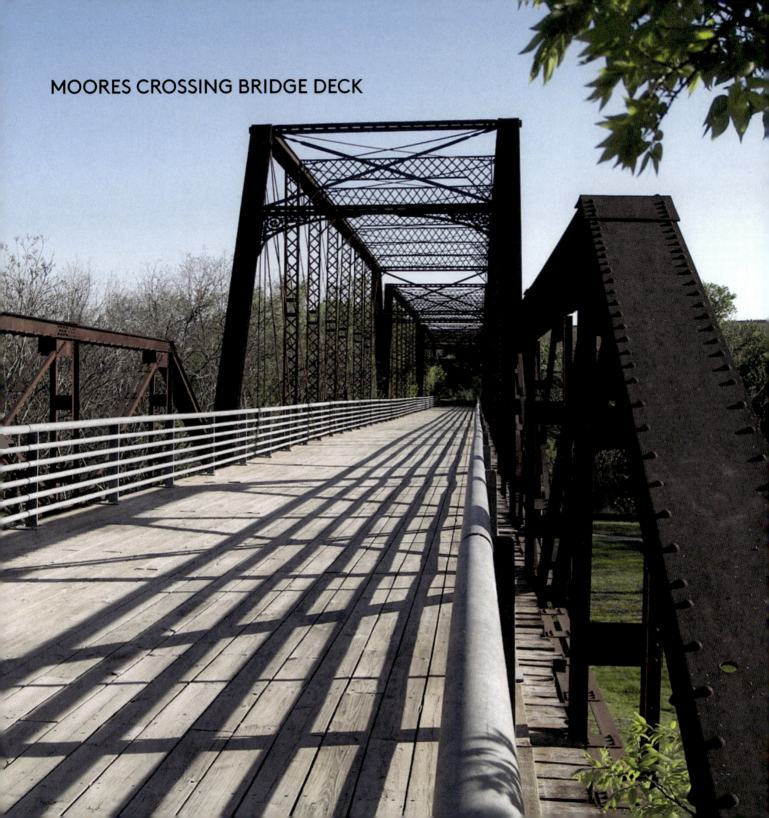

MOORES CROSSING BRIDGE DECK

Factors that need to be considered when creating the proper structure for a bridge are:

- The length that the bridge needs to span

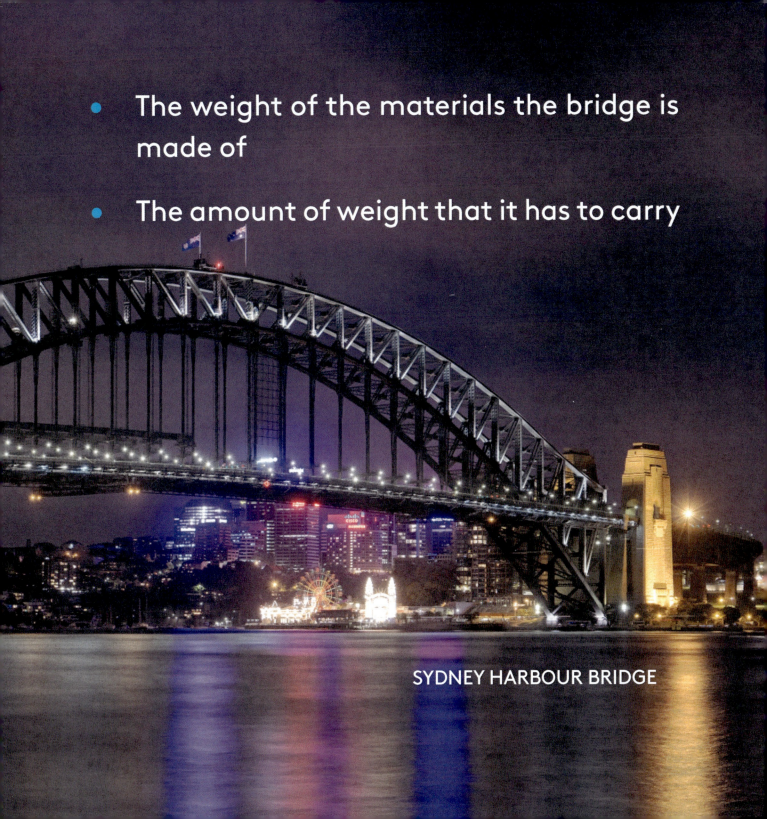

- The weight of the materials the bridge is made of

- The amount of weight that it has to carry

SYDNEY HARBOUR BRIDGE

A COLLAPSED BRIDGE AFTER AN EARTHQUAKE

Bridges do collapse once in a while. For example, a severe earthquake can cause a bridge to collapse.

However, most modern bridges are built with the best architectural designs, engineering, and construction so that people and their vehicles stay safe.

Architects and engineers who build bridges must balance several different types of forces to ensure that the bridges are sturdy. There are two main kinds of forces: compression, which is a pushing force that acts inward, and tension, which is a pulling force that acts outward. The engineers also have to make sure that the load the bridge carries is balanced on abutments, which are supports at its sides, and piers, which are supports under the middle of the bridge.

In addition to carrying its own weight, called the dead load, the bridge has to carry different amounts of weight from cars, trains, or people, called the live load. These loads increase the forces on the bridge. For example, if a bridge is designed for trains, it flexes to accommodate the heavy weight of the trains that pass over it.

HAMMERSMITH BRIDGE
AND RIVERSIDE

TSUNAMI IS ABOUT TO HIT THE BRIDGE

ENVIRONMENTAL FORCES

Along with the weight that bridges must carry, they also have to be able to withstand environmental forces. Bridges that span rivers sometimes have water that backs up behind them. Their abutments are often built with openings that allow floodwaters to pass through. Heavy gusts of wind can cause problems for the stability of bridges as well. Wind can cause torsion, which is a type of twisting force, on the deck of the bridge.

Modern bridges have sections that have been tested in wind tunnels. Their decks are reinforced with heavy trusses, which are diagonal bars that form triangles at the bridge's sides.

BEAM BRIDGE

ARCH BRIDGE

TYPES OF BRIDGES

Architects and engineers choose the design of a bridge based on its function as well as its overall environment. The basic designs can be modified and combinations of the different styles can be used within the same bridge.

- **Beam Bridges** are easy to build, but they have a limited span. An example is the Lake Pontchartrain Causeway in Louisiana.

- **Arch Bridges** are very strong, but expensive to build. An example is the Charles Bridge in Prague.

- **Truss Bridges** are frequently used as a drawbridge or overpass for trains and are difficult to construct. An example is the George Street Bridge in Aurora, Indiana.

QUEENSBORO BRIDGE

- **Cantilever Bridges** are ideal for rivers that are prone to flooding, but are also very difficult to construct. An example is the Queensboro Bridge in New York City.

GOLDEN GATE BRIDGE

- **Suspension Bridges** can span up to 7,000 feet, but are expensive, and take a long time and a great deal of material to build. An example is the Golden Gate Bridge in San Francisco.

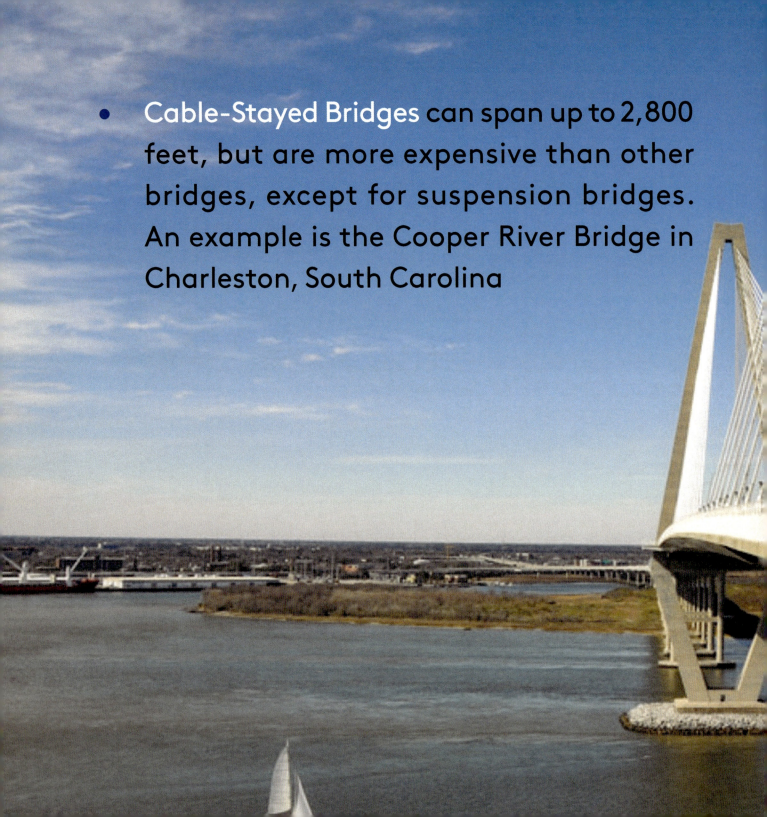

- **Cable-Stayed Bridges** can span up to 2,800 feet, but are more expensive than other bridges, except for suspension bridges. An example is the Cooper River Bridge in Charleston, South Carolina

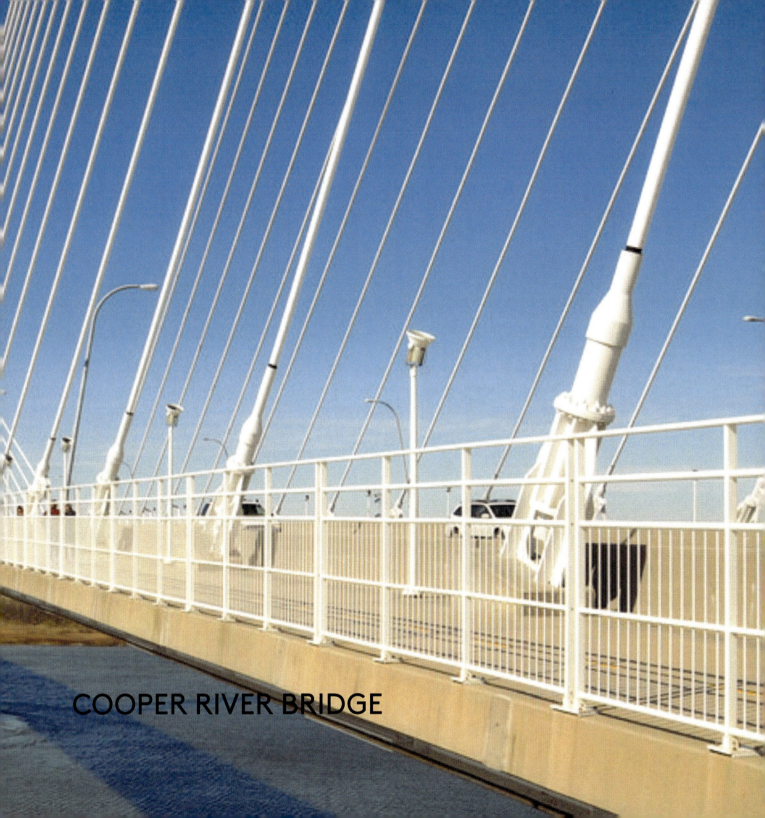

COOPER RIVER BRIDGE

TUNNELS

A tunnel is a long horizontal tube that is excavated or hollowed out of stone or soil. Building a tunnel that doesn't collapse is one of the most challenging construction projects for a civil engineer. Many tunnels are considered to be masterpieces of technology. Tunnels are used for trains, for highways, for public utilities, and for telecommunications.

There are lots of different methods used to take out or excavate the soil or stone needed to make a manmade tunnel. Tunnels are excavated by:

- Using manual labor

- Setting off explosives

- Rapidly heating and cooling, and

- Using special equipment that bores through the rock

Sometimes a combination of these methods is used.

HINDHEAD TUNNEL
CONSTRUCTION

TUNNEL PORTAL

PARTS OF A TUNNEL

Just like arches are used to make well-constructed bridges, arches are also used in tunnel construction. In fact, a tunnel is just one continuous arch. If you are driving on the highway and come across a tunnel, you will drive through the tunnel's opening, which is called a portal.

The top section of the tube is called its crown and the bottom section is called its invert. Tunnel engineers work with the same forces that bridge engineers do.

They must use very strong materials such as steel, concrete, and iron to deal with the forces of tension, compression, shearing, and torsion. Tunnels also have dead loads and live loads, just like bridges.

MINING UNDERGROUND TUNNEL

TYPES OF TUNNELS

There are three main types of tunnels: mining tunnels, public works or utility tunnels, and transportation tunnels. Mining tunnels are used so that miners can get deep inside the ground to extract metal deposits for use in industry. They cost less to build than the other two types of tunnels, but unfortunately they're not as safe.

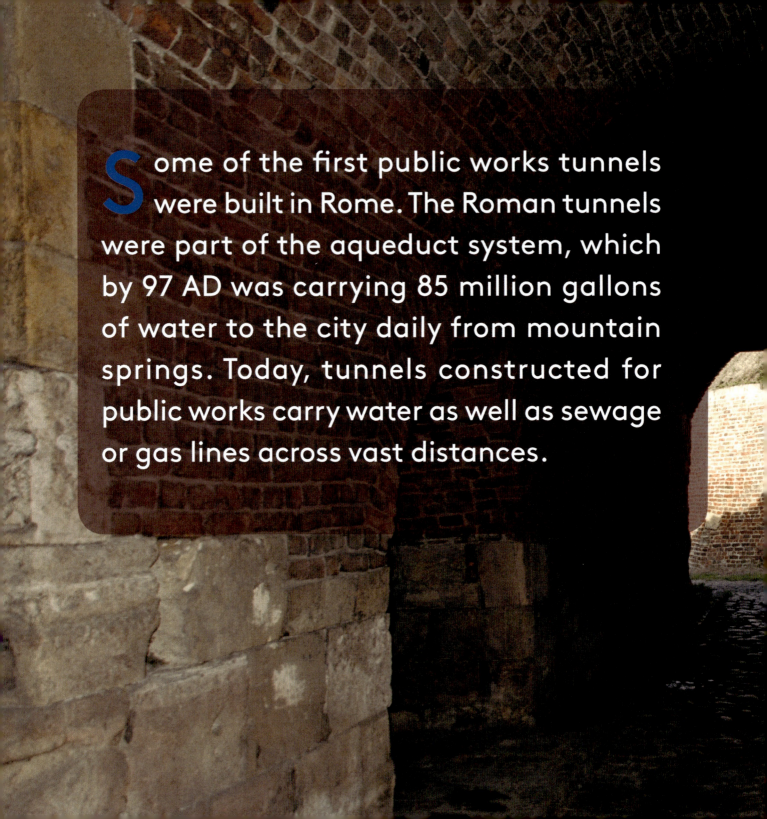

Some of the first public works tunnels were built in Rome. The Roman tunnels were part of the aqueduct system, which by 97 AD was carrying 85 million gallons of water to the city daily from mountain springs. Today, tunnels constructed for public works carry water as well as sewage or gas lines across vast distances.

OLD ROMAN TUNNEL

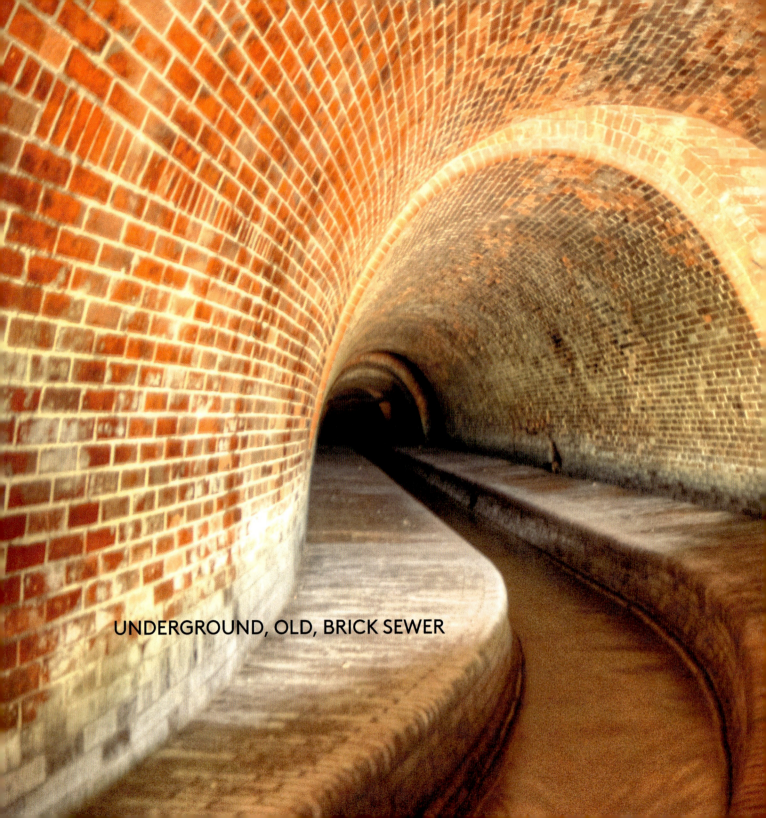

UNDERGROUND, OLD, BRICK SEWER

Before the advent of trains and automobiles, there were canals, which were artificial waterways for shipping. They usually were built above ground, but sometimes if a mountain was in the way, an underground canal had to be built. This type of construction is what led to the development of transportation tunnels. One of the first tunnels designed for cars was the Holland Tunnel, which was built in 1927 and connects New York City to New Jersey.

Other famous transportation tunnels include:

- The Gotthard Base Tunnel in Switzerland, designed for railways
- The Yerba Buena Island Tunnel in California, designed for cars
- The Lærdal Tunnel in Norway, designed for cars
- The Aizhai Extra Large Suspension Bridge in China, designed for cars
- The Channel Tunnel under the English Channel, designed for railways
- The Seikan Tunnel in Japan, designed for railways

青函隧道

SEIKAN TUNNEL IN JAPAN

CITYSCAPE

BUILDINGS

As space in cities gets more and more filled, architects and engineers are being challenged to create taller and taller buildings, called skyscrapers. These types of buildings are popular because they have lots of space for homes or offices inside even though they don't take up that much room on the ground. Before builders learned how to build underground foundations, taller buildings had thicker walls on their lower floors to combat the weight of the upper floors.

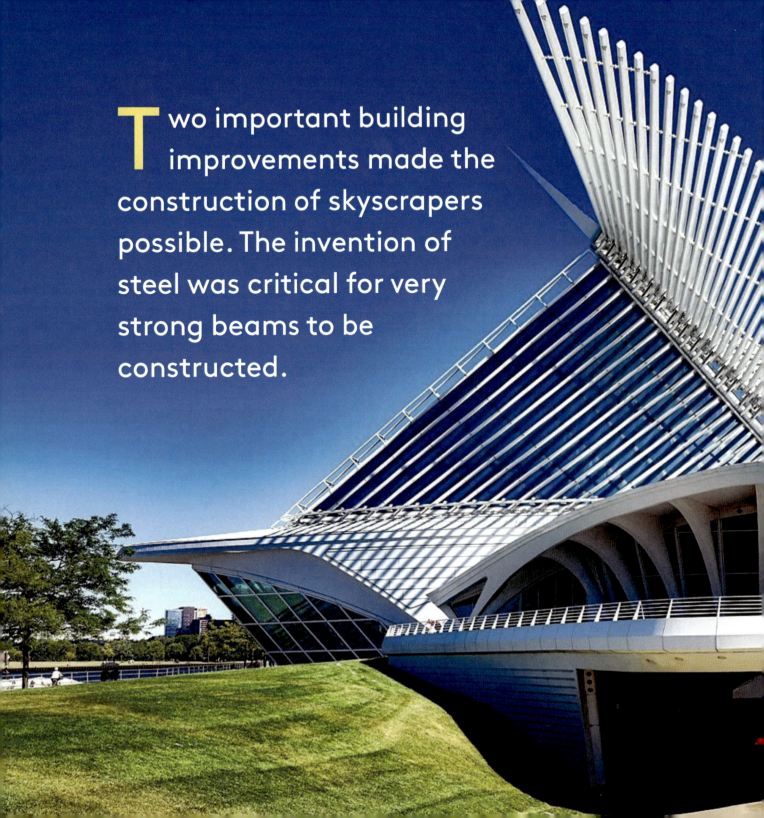

Two important building improvements made the construction of skyscrapers possible. The invention of steel was critical for very strong beams to be constructed.

The other important invention was the elevator so that people could travel safely from floor to floor without having to walk up many flights of stairs. Today, skyscrapers are constructed in two parts. Below the ground, the foundation is built. If the building is constructed in a city that has earthquakes, it's built on a foundation that can move, so that the building and people in it will survive the shaking.

ELEVATOR

Even buildings with hundreds of floors can sway back and forth a few feet so they won't get severely damaged during an earthquake.

Once the foundation is built, the superstructure above the ground is put in place. Enormous cranes are used to get the steel frame pieces into the proper position so they can be bolted together.

As the skyscraper is built, workers put in the floors and hang the outer walls. The entire structure must be complete before any of the inside systems are installed.

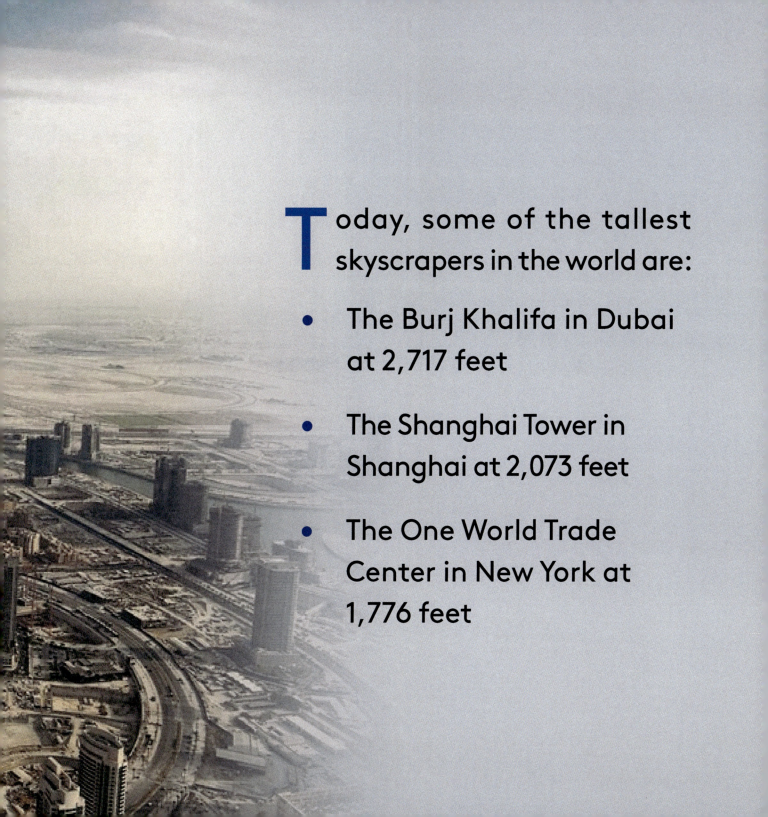

Today, some of the tallest skyscrapers in the world are:

- The Burj Khalifa in Dubai at 2,717 feet

- The Shanghai Tower in Shanghai at 2,073 feet

- The One World Trade Center in New York at 1,776 feet

SUMMARY

Architects and engineers who design and build bridges, tunnels, and buildings have unique challenges. They must ensure that their structures are safe for people, vehicles, and freight. In addition to the force of gravity, they must deal with compression, tension, and torsion. Modern bridges, tunnels, and buildings are masterpieces of technology.

Awesome! Now that you know more about how some landmarks are built you can read more information about one of the most famous landmarks in the Baby Professor book *Interesting Facts about the Empire State Building.*

Visit

BABY PROFESSOR
EDUCATION KIDS

www.BabyProfessorBooks.com

to download Free Baby Professor eBooks
and view our catalog of new and exciting
Children's Books

Made in the USA
Monee, IL
13 September 2021